Eastern Daily Press

Images of Norfolk

Eastern Daily Press

Images of Norfolk

The Breedon Books
Publishing Company
Derby

First published in Great Britain by
The Breedon Books Publishing Company Limited
44 Friar Gate, Derby, DE1 1DA.
1995

Dedication
To the staff photographers and librarians throughout the years.

Acknowledgements
We would like to thank the Eastern Counties Newspapers'
photographic department, and especially Diane Townsend and
Jackie Burrows. Chief librarian Rosemary Dixon and her team of
Frances Pearce, Joy Wright and Alison Maloney have given much
help. Ken Arnott and Pat Midgley gave valuable information on
particular pictures. Our thanks also, to John Hocknell and Brian
Waite for guiding us to undiscovered gems. To our wives, Velma
and Hazel, for tolerating our disruption of their domestic routines.
And, finally, a special thank you to Steve Snelling for his sound
advice and enthusiasm.

Photographs
Reproductions of any of the photographs featured in this book can
be purchased from Eastern Counties Newspapers' head office at
Prospect House, Rouen Road, Norwich.

ISBN 1 885983 035 8

Printed and bound by Butler & Tanner, Frome, Somerset.
Jacket printed by Premier Print, Nottingham.
Colour separations by Colour Services, Leicester.

Contents

Introduction

NORFOLK is special. And you don't need to be a true-born Norfolkman to realise that. Just ask any one of the hundreds of thousands of holidaymakers and day trippers who flock to the county each year. The wide-open skies, the long and varied coastline, the 1.3 million-plus acres of infinite variety beckon irresistibly to newcomers and natives alike.

Norfolk is one of the great regional centres of England, up there with the Cornwalls, Tynesides and Yorkshires. The 65 miles from Walpole Cross Keys in the west to Yarmouth in the east is a slice of England rich in history and landscape. The typical Norfolkman is not given to sounding off about how wonderful his county is; he knows. And like those other great regional centres, Norfolk has its own great regional paper. The *Eastern Daily Press* is consistently the best-selling paper in East Anglia – and frequently the best-selling regional morning paper in the country too. For thousands of Norfolk people it is as much a part of local life as Cromer crabs, the Broads or Norwich City FC.

The *EDP* has been essential reading since it began publishing in 1870, recording faithfully the dramas and the minutiae of Norfolk life.

The newspaper has been there to cover great disasters – and the village fête; Royal visits – or harvesting; plane crashes – or just plain enjoyment. In short, the ordinary and the extraordinary.

The quality of *EDP* photographs is legendary, and the choice of the final 300 or so pictures has been no easy task.

Norfolk's position out on a geographical limb jutting into the North Sea has been reflected in the independent character of its people throughout the county's long and eventful history. From Boudicca (Boadicea) onwards, Norfolk people have shown that they like their own ways very much, thank you. Not for nothing is the county's motto 'Dew Diff'rent'.

Although we have divided the contents of this book into many headings, two themes dominate: the sea and the land. The character of Norfolk is partly shaped by its landscape. Rich farmland, the Brecks, the Broads, land painfully reclaimed from river and sea.

The North Sea provides a rich harvest for the county. But Norfolk people have never been able to forget that it also, in the words of Henry James, 'moves for ever, like a ruminating beast'. Along the 90 miles of the county's coastline, it is constantly testing man's ingenuity and pretensions at taming it. Sometimes, as in 1953 and 1978, nature has gained the upper hand in a dramatic and terrible fashion.

And, naturally, the *EDP* has been there to record it.

This book has tried to complement the earlier title in this series, the *Evening News* book, *Images of Norwich*. For one thing, we have begun our survey exactly as the official city boundary ends and the rest of the county begins.

Our pictures are drawn from living memory, concentrating on the eventful decades of the 1940s, 1950s and 1960s, but there are entries from other times too.

This is not the story of famous people – although well-known faces do crop up – but the ordinary people of Norfolk, the backbone of the county. We have also featured some of the buildings – historic and modern – inextricably bound up with the story of Norfolk.

On very few occasions were these historic pictures taken with some distant posterity in mind. Street scenes, for example, taken for the most prosaic of reasons, have aged gracefully with the patina of nostalgia, and sometimes poignancy when the scene they depict has since been swept away by development.

A chance photograph of a country scene, taken because it caught the sharp eye of an *EDP* photographer travelling between 'jobs', takes on a rich historic significance because it records the passing of a way of life.

We stand and watch a young boy taking

careful aim at a coconut shy at his village fête; we share the concentration of a country craftsman absorbed in his timeless skill; we see the grins as families arrive for their long-awaited annual holiday at Yarmouth; we witness the drawn and grim faces of local families struggling to come to terms with the enormity of a flood disaster. Our aim has been to paint a picture of Norfolk people at work, rest and play.

We have chosen some pictures because of the extraordinary stories behind them, and others because they marked some turning point in the county's way of life.

We have dedicated this book to all the photographers who have worked for Eastern Counties Newspapers or its earlier incarnation as the Norfolk News Company. It is a truism but one worth stating that without them and their skill, sympathy for their subject and uncanny flair for a memorable picture, this project would have been nothing.

With even the wide range of pictures in this book we can only paint a tiny corner of the rich canvas that is Norfolk. There are many more gems waiting to be discovered in the *EDP's* matchless archives, of that we are certain.

But taken as a whole, these pictures will, we hope, convey much of that essential, unquantifiable, immeasurable specialness that truly makes Norfolk 'diff'rent'.

Sir John Betjeman wrote in 1958, as apposite as ever: 'These Norfolk lanes recall lost innocence.' We invite you to step with us down those lanes once more.

We hope you enjoy your journey.

Trevor Heaton
Alan Atherton

Royal Norfolk

'Dear old Sandringham, the place I love better than anywhere else in the world,' wrote King George V, and his son George VI wrote in similar vein, 'I love the place.' Sandringham, which was bought by the future Edward VII in 1862, has remained a favourite retreat of the Royal Family to this day. The Royal Family cherish Sandringham as a sanctuary of peace and quiet – but that does not mean they do not play their full part in the local community. Generations of monarchs have carried out their duties as head of the huge Sandringham Estate with enthusiasm and foresight. Norfolk has also been the focus of many royal visits through the years, and our opening selection of pictures celebrates the county's very special royal links.

Prince Henry, later the Duke of Gloucester, inspecting a guard of honour at a Scout jamboree held at Crown Point in May 1922.

The King and Queen and the two princesses are shown leaving Sandringham Church on 29 June 1947 after the laying-up by the King of the colours of the 1st Battalion, Royal Norfolk Regiment.

Queen in waiting: the then Princess Elizabeth with her sister Princess Margaret join their parents King George VI and Queen Elizabeth at a Sandringham Garden Party given on 13 July 1946 to nearly 3,000 tenants and workers on the Royal estate.

The Queen Mother has long been an enthusiastic patron of the arts and is especially associated with the King's Lynn Festival, founded in 1951 by her lady-in-waiting Ruth, Lady Fermoy (seen in the centre of this picture). Two years earlier, the *EDP* attended a reception when the pianist Alfred Cortot was received by the then Queen Elizabeth, Queen Mary and the Mayor of Lynn, Mr H.B.Fisher.

Princess Margaret, their Commissioner-in-Chief, had a special smile for these three very small cadets during an inspection of units of the St John Ambulance Brigade at Sennowe Park in July 1950. In the background is Lieutenant Colonel Sir Thomas Cook (County Commissioner).

The Princess Royal (Princess Mary) inspecting the Women's Royal Army Corps radar operators during her visit to Weybourne Anti-Aircraft Camp in August 1951.

Queen Mary and the Princess Royal at a fête in the grounds of Sandringham rectory during 1951.

On 11 February 1952 crowds (together with the world's newsreel and Press representatives) watch the royal train carrying the late King's body leave Wolferton for London. George VI was born at Sandringham on 14 December 1895; on 6 February 1952 he died there.

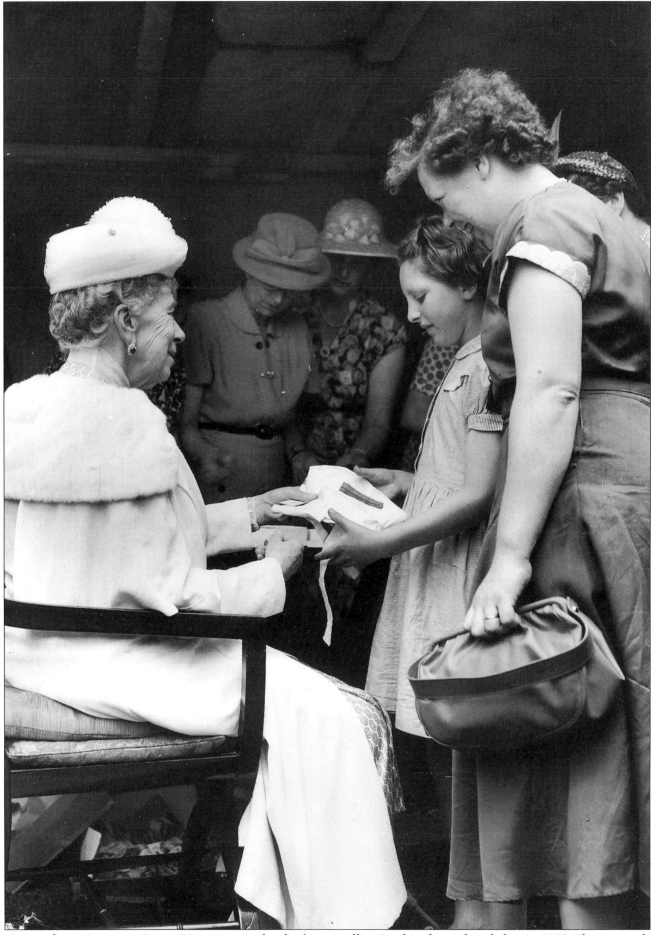

By royal appointment: Queen Mary seen at the the fancy stall at Sandringham church fête in 1952. She manned
the stall for one and a half hours, selling items ranging from 3d pencils to a red velvet handbag for 35/-.
The royal takings? £55.

The number of West Norfolk businesses boasting 'by Royal appointment' signs testifies to the way the Royal Family has played its own part in supporting local traders over the years. And every now and then, as in this 29 August 1952 picture of Queen Mary leaving King's Lynn store Jermyns, a royal visitor may arrive in person.

The Queen, accompanied by the Duke of Edinburgh, visits one of the victims of the East Coast floods in 1953 at King's Lynn.

Proud day: The Queen Mother walks with the Mayor of King's Lynn, Mr B.Bremner on 26 July 1954, followed by Princess Margaret. The Queen Mother was at Lynn to receive the Freedom of the Borough, the first woman to do so. Forty years later she returned to Lynn for an anniversary celebration in which she spoke of her affection for 'this dear old town'.

The young Prince Charles and Princess Anne take a keen interest in the West Norfolk Foxhounds at a meet on 12 January 1956.

The Queen seen sharing a joke at a point-to-point held at Sporle on 28 April 1956.

Princess Anne performed her first 'official' public engagement at the age of nine years. In January 1960, deputising for the Queen, she distributed the prizes at West Newton Sunday School. Here she hands over a prize to Linda Jakeman while Prince Charles looks on from a seat by the piano.

Wing Commander C.H.T.Pennal, officer commanding the Engineering Wing, points out some of the finer points of a Lightning aircraft to the Duchess of Gloucester when she is shown round a hanger during her visit to RAF Coltishall in June 1967.

The Royal Family arrives at King's Lynn railway station on 29 December 1967 for their Sandringham holiday. Escorted by station manager Mr R.C.Macfarlane, one notable absentee from the royal party was the Duke of Edinburgh, who was still in London, recovering from a wrist operation.

Prince Charles and Princess Anne leave King's Lynn station in December 1967 on their way to Sandringham for the New Year.

Lady Sarah Armstrong-Jones and Prince Edward are followed by Viscount Linley and Prince Andrew on 22 January 1968 when they arrived at King's Lynn railway station with Princess Margaret to journey back to London after the Royal Family's traditional holiday at Sandringham.

Prince Michael of Kent (centre), who took part in the Lancia Pointer Midsummer Stages Rally, chatting to his co-driver and friend in June 1973.

1972 and an unmistakable Lady Diana Spencer poses for the *EDP* camera at the Sandringham Flower Show pet show. When this picture was republished to celebrate the royal engagement it excited world-wide interest.

The Duke of Kent looks at the heart of the matter as he examines the engine of a Lotus sports car being built at the company's Hethel plant in March 1976. Accompanying him on his tour, and explaining the finer details, is Colin Chapman.

The Duke of Gloucester at Banham International Motor Museum where he tries out a 1954 Mercedes Benz 300 SL. He was shown round in April 1977 by the museum's owner, Lord Cranworth.

Above: The Duke of Edinburgh brings out smiles as he chats with a crowd of employees at Anglia Canners, during a tour of King's Lynn factories in November 1978.

Above: There have been Norfolk visits by other royals, of course. In this picture Princess Margaretha of Sweden opens the huge Northern Cold Storage plant (now Frigoscandia) on the outskirts of King's Lynn on 16 October 1965. Her husband, John Ambler, is pictured alongside her.

Left: Anmer, until recently the home of the Duke and Duchess of Kent, has always been one of the quieter villages on the Royal Estate. In 1958 the *EDP* pictured farmworkers Stanley 'Tom' Ockley JP, and his nephew, Douglas Whitmore, admiring the new Harry Carter-carved village sign, a gift to the Queen from the Norfolk Boy Scouts' Association.

Oh we do like to be beside the Seaside

Think of Norfolk, and holidays by the sea are never far from mind. The county's 90 miles of coastline and numerous sandy beaches have proved a magnet for tourists for more than 100 years. The building of rail links to Hunstanton, Cromer and Yarmouth in the last century brought millions of potential holidaymakers within an easy train ride of the coast. Great Yarmouth, or Yarmouth as it is simply known in the county, has developed into one of the country's leading resorts, with miles of entertainment and 200 acres of sandy beaches. Smaller, but still hugely popular, are resorts such as Hunstanton ('Sunny Hunny') and Cromer.

In July 1962 coaches from around Britain disgorge their holiday passengers at the former Yarmouth Beach railway station (notice the old platforms). The holidaymakers then waited for Corporation Transport buses to take them to their hotels and boarding houses. Buses on D and E services only operated on Saturdays.

Yarmouth's 'Golden Mile' with the Winter Gardens and Wellington Pier, the Jetty, and, in the distance, the Britannia Pier.

High tea at Mrs Hall's Brittwell Guest House, Great Yarmouth, in July 1952.

Playing beach cricket whilst on holiday at Hemsby *c.*1960 are the Tinkler family from Norwich.

Bronco bikes at
Yarmouth Pleasure
Beach in September
1953.

Children having fun on the
pedal car race track at Yarmouth
in July 1957. At the Wellington
Pier Theatre (behind) Benny Hill
was staging his summer show.

Mr David Griffiths, from Bristol, inspires children to model in sand at Cromer as he goes to work on a second animal after completing this large elephant in August 1971.

The more peaceful side of Great Yarmouth, pictured in August 1960.

The newly-installed Guinness Festival clock attracted large crowds at Yarmouth in May 1955. The clock struck each 15 minutes.

A typical busy holiday weekend at Hunstanton, 'Sunny Hunny'. This picture was taken Whit Sunday, 1959. Hunstanton's success as a seaside resort was founded on the vision of the Le Strange family and the railway links which enabled hundreds of day trippers to come from Peterborough and further afield. Walter Rye, that famous Norfolk writer, complained in 1889: "The old town was once a pleasant watering hole like Cromer, but has been to a great extent spoiled by the railway, which brings to it crowds of excursionists from Northampton and elsewhere." But the hundreds of thousands of visitors before and after his words have begged to differ.

Whit Monday 1965 on Yarmouth's 'Golden Mile'. For 9/- holidaymakers could take a tour to Aldeburgh-on-Sea and Dunwich ruins. On the right of the picture is the Grotto Castle and Aquazoo.

Fun in the Wellington Pier Gardens at Great Yarmouth riding on the '*News Chronicle* Special'. Watching is the typical schoolboy in cap and double-breasted raincoat.

This Great Yarmouth Corporation Transport's Coronation Coach won first prize in the Coronation Day procession in June 1953. The AEC bus, with open platform and open upper deck, ran throughout the season giving rides along the sea front.

Where would a visit to the seaside be without a donkey ride? These donkeys – Jenny, Noddy, Bruno, Johnny, Flicker, Inky, Shaggy, Jerry and Billy – were working on Hunstanton beach in the summer of 1963 when this picture was taken. Geoffrey Searle began the tradition in 1936.

What a seaside holiday is all about!
Two ladies keeping cool on a summer's
day in July 1965 at Yarmouth.

Britannia Pier, Yarmouth, in the
early part of the century. The
helter-skelter, known as The
Mat, was rescued when the pier
was set on fire by Suffragettes in
1914. It was re-erected on the
bank of the River Thurne at
Potter Heigham as a holiday
cottage with the name 'Dutch
Tutch'. Rowley's Grand Variety
Company and Ethel Cadman
were entertaining on the pier at
the time of this picture.

Holiday crowds enjoying the beach, promenade and concert at Yarmouth.

Mrs Hall, proprietress of the Brittwell Guest House in Nelson Road Central, waves goodbye to holidaymakers
who had spent their week or fortnight with her in Great Yarmouth in July 1952.

A Time to Reap, A Time to Sow

The modern farming history of Norfolk really begins with the innovator 'Turnip' Townshend, and aided by a rich and diverse landscape the county has grown to be one of England's foremost agricultural counties. Crops as diverse as wheat and lavender, barley and beet, and latterly oil seed rape and linseed are testament to the largess which nature has bestowed on the county.

In fact, so wide and fruitful is the range of crops that many people have claimed Norfolk could easily be self sufficient.

We have arranged this section in the order of the seasons to show that, whether farming is down to horsepower or mechanical, the natural rhythm of the year never changes.

The blessing of the plough on Plough Sunday took place on the first Sunday after the Twelve Days of Christmas, as in this 7 January 1950 service at Swaffham's Ss Peter and Paul Church. The 'winter warmer' of plough pudding is traditional fare on this day in Norfolk.

Mechanical power was supplanting horsepower by the 1950s. Yet even in 1959 they could still be found on many farms. Dinah is carrying out her first job of the year (20 February) – strawberry hoeing – helped by her owner, Mr R.Gunns of Goldpit Farm, Stow Bridge.

From surrounding farms, many of which were completely frozen-up, farm workers gathered at The Greens, Hempnall, to fill up with water for their farm stock from a standpipe operated by men of Depwade Rural District Council's water department in February 1963.

Seed in one side and Fison's No.5 fertiliser in the other of this Massey Harris combine drill as preparations are made for the Spring sowing in February 1953.

Nowadays the Grimston Road at South Wootton, seen here in the background of this 1952 picture, is a busy conduit for commuter traffic into King's Lynn. But things were altogether more peaceful when the *EDP* pictured workers at Mr J.Lee's smallholding planting seed potatoes.

Norfolk author George Borrow painted a romanticised image of gypsies in such works as *Romany Rye*. The reality has always been tougher for the travellers, who have played an important role for generations in Norfolk agriculture through their seasonal work. This 1951 picture was taken in the Thetford area.

Strawberries and cream are an essential part of British summers and Norfolk strawberries are some of the best in the country. In this 1968 view, taken near King's Lynn, one very junior consumer samples some of the goodies on offer.

Haymaking at Swanton Morley aerodrome in July 1958. The baler at the rear bears the name P.A.Vincent, Manor Farm, Rackheath.

In July 1954, 400 Yorkshire members of the National Union of Agricultural Workers gathered in Fakenham cemetery to pay tribute to Sir George Edwards, who founded their union in 1906. Mr Edwin Gooch, the president, is seen addressing the group after laying a wreath on Sir George's grave.

Coals to Newcastle: Selected strains were grown in the nurseries of Roudham Farms Ltd to replace diseased stock in the hop gardens of Kent. As many as 70,000 plants were sent out each year from Thetford.

Mr P. de la Cour's men thresh and bale coltsfoot at Haugh Farm, Banham in August 1962. The top of the shocks of the grass were bound with twine to prevent the seed being blown out by the wind.

The day of the horse was far from over at Hall Farm, West Barsham where Mr J.A.Keith had 12 Suffolks still at work. Nine of them are seen here in August 1955 during a break from stacking peas and oats.

Gleaning among the stubble a woman and two children seek grain for their poultry.

Muck-spreading the lazy way with a mechanical manure spreader drawn by a tractor in September 1956.

With their flint bases to keep out rats and mice, and their overhanging thatch, these round stacks of wheat and oats, pictured in September 1952 on Mr Gaze's Brewery Farm, Diss are of a type seldom seen. Ever since the Gaze family moved into Brewery Farm in 1883 they were built this way, and for 50 years were thatched by Mr Jack Last and his father before him. The circular emblem on the top of each stack was their own particular trademark.

A demonstration arranged by Norfolk Farm Machinery Club, in conjunction with the National Agricultural Advisory Service, to show owners and operators of sugar beet harvesters how machines should be set and adjusted. This picture taken in September 1956 shows a GBW harvester at work on Messrs L.F. & H.F.Harrison's Manor Farm, Brandon Parva topping, lifting and loading the beet in one operation.

Mr Walter Pestell topping sugar beet the old way at Barton Farm, Sea Palling in October 1957.

Field work has been an important part of the Norfolk economy for generations. Three women take a second off their back-breaking task of lifting carrots in a field near King's Lynn to pose for the *EDP* camera in late October 1957.

When harvest time beckons, it's all hands to the pumps. That remains as true today as in this vintage picture of the Walker family gathering in the mangolds at Warren Lodge Farm, Methwold. George Walker, his wife and three daughters – Ellen, Eileen and Muriel – and Jack Walker pitch in.

Norfolk farming innovation emerged yet again in the development of sugar beet as a major crop. Cantley was the first beet sugar factory in England, to be followed by sites at King's Lynn and Wissington. Wissington has recently enjoyed a £50 million expansion programme; as a consequence Lynn's Saddlebow plant closed in 1994. The *EDP* captured the dramatic swirls of steam at the Saddlebow factory on 9 December 1964.

Heacham ploughman Tom Rout was puzzled when he ploughed up a twisted piece of metal in November 1950 at Ken Hill, Snettisham. The metal turned out to be a priceless gold alloy torc dating back 2,000 years. Village historian John Bingham wrote in 1989: 'Until it is quite certain that this harvest has been completed, there will be no field in the land which is ploughed and tended with such assiduous care, and meticulous scrutiny.' He was right; only a few years later an amateur archaeologist uncovered the most fabulous finds of all, now in the British Museum.

War and Peace

It was the invention of air-power – and the recognition that the main threat to British security came from Germany rather than France – which led to the development of the county's bases. In fact, the strategic importance of the county was realised as far back as January 1915 when the first air-raid ever on British soil took the form of a Zeppelin attack on Yarmouth and King's Lynn. But as world war gave way to cold war, Norfolk still had a role to play. Our selection opens with a look at the huge Stanford Battle Training Area in Breckland and a poignant view of Norfolk's most secret – and ghostly – village. We dedicate this section to the brave men and women who have served the county at home or overseas in all branches of the Services.

In 1942 the War Office ordered a complete evacuation at short notice as Tottington village was to be included in the training area. Fourteen years later in May 1956 it was to look like this.

The round-towered All Saints' Church at Stanford is protected from the battle zone by a 6ft wire fence and the window openings are filled with corrugated iron sheets..

Time for a brew-up for soldiers of the Royal Tank Regiment in 1949.

Tanks seek out their 'enemy' whilst on manoeuvres in the Battle Area in 1949.

Establishing radio contact while on manoeuvres in the Battle Area.

The all-important 'traffic cop' has everything under control as another group of vehicles arrives for exercises at the Stanford Battle Training Area.

Wearing the kilt of the 1st Battalion, Queen's Own Cameron Highlanders, of which he is Colonel-in-Chief, the Duke of Edinburgh arrives at Stanford Battle Area to inspect his troops on exercise in June 1958.

Army Cadets search through waist-high bracken looking for hidden 'enemy' soldiers. In July 1953, 4,500 cadets were on a week-long camp at the Battle Training Area and they came from schools in East and Southern England.

A Caterpillar D2 bulldozer operated by Mr L.Draper filling in gunsite holes and slit trenches near Cockley Cley.

The hospital supply depot at Coltishall Hall had a machine room, cutting-out room and an aseptic swab room. Forty workers attached to the depot attended two or three times a week to prepare supplies for sick and wounded soldiers and for air-raid casualties. This photograph, taken in November 1939, shows some of them at work. There were 77 such depots in Norfolk.

Destruction caused by a land-mine which fell on Middlegate Street, Yarmouth, in April 1941.

A concrete gun-
mounting stands in
front of the pill box
made from the shell
of an old wind pump
near Ludham Bridge.

Mr David Anderson and Miss
Diana Harrod of Thorpe look at
the graves in July 1954 of German
airmen brought down at the
beginning of the war at
Happisburgh.

Captain C.L.Ashurst explains map reading to women Home Guard at Dereham. Behind him are (left to right) Miss Balbrook, Miss Williamson, Park, Miss Williamson and Mrs Roper in June 1954. Perhaps the two Misses Williamson are sisters.

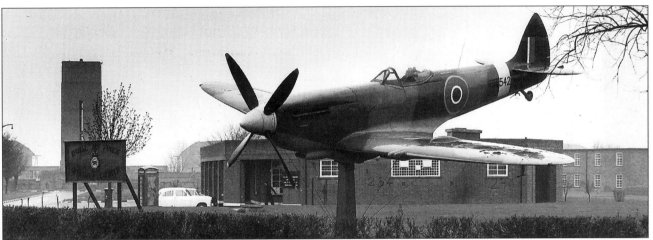

The Spitfire which stood at the entrance to RAF Horsham St Faith. Behind it is the main guardroom, and in the distance the hangers, barrack blocks and water tower which has recently been demolished.When an Anson aircraft of the Communications Flight took off in the morning of 29 April 1963 it brought to an end 20 years of RAF history at the station. The runways are now used as Norwich Airport.

Members of the Direct Action Committee Against Nuclear War picket the Thor missile base at North Pickenham in south-west Norfolk in November 1958.

RAF Marham has long played a key role in the defence of this country and our allies. And many famous aircraft have flown in over the years, ranging from Tornados, Nimrods and Victors to Wellingtons, B29s and B50s. Valiant bombers were stationed here in the 1950s and 1960s, but perhaps the most awe-inspiring visitors have been the B52 Strato Fortresses. Two United States aircrew pose for the *EDP* lens in front of the giant eight-engined bomber.

The arrival of thousands of American servicemen in Norfolk during World War Two and after made an undoubted cultural impact on the inhabitants. But culture is a two-way thing and many Americans discovered a liking for English drizzle, warm beer and 'Olde England'. Sculthorpe serviceman Captain Phil Ooley, who lived at Dersingham, had a taste for vintage cycles. Captain Ooley and his penny-farthing are pictured on 29 April 1957 with Dersingham resident Sonny Skipper outside the village's former White Horse pub.

The Happiest Days of Your Life

Well, they're not always, are they? But there are few of us who do not look back on our schooldays with affection. Here is a selection of pure nostalgia – and a little genuine history too.

RAF police from RAF Horsham St Faith (now Norwich Airport) give some King's Lynn pupils road safety lessons in 1949 or 1950. Then-sergeant Jim Baker, of South Wootton (pictured left) recalled how one little boy refused to go with the nice policemen – and ended up being scolded by his mum (you can see the scolding on the right of the picture).

Back to the days when balsa, Meccano and Airfix were king, with this evocative 1950s study of a handicraft class at Hamond's Grammar School at Swaffham.

A singsong at Fakenham Nursery School, where the principal, Miss Marjorie McAnally, taught local and American children from three to five years of age.

The strike of Burston schoolchildren started in 1914 when Mr Tom Higdon, a pioneer of the National Union of Agricultural Workers in Norfolk and a full-blooded socialist, and Annie, his wife, were dismissed from their posts as teachers at Burston Village School. When funds were made available through union activity the 'Strike School' was built and Mr and Mrs Higdon continued as teachers. In 1939 Mr Higdon died, Annie retired and the pupils returned to the village school. This photograph, taken in November 1961, shows the front of the building which is covered with inscriptions listing those who contributed the fund.

Not a power tool in sight... a 1950s woodworking class busy in Swaffham Shirehall and captured by the *EDP* camera lens.

Part of the charming world of childhood fantasy was vividly captured for Diss Church School infants by the gift in January 1953 of a model depicting characters, scenes and incidents from eight nursery rhymes. The model was the gift of Lieutenant A.Schoepke, of the United States Air Force, who in civilian life was a display artist. He made it for his two small sons as a background to the Christmas tree.

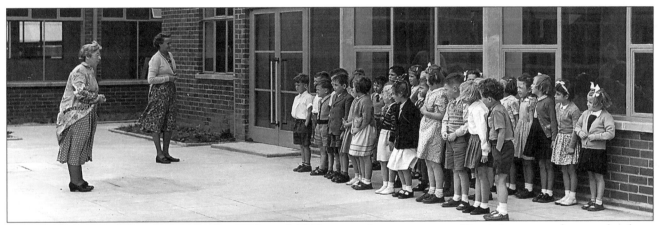

Slum clearance and expansion in the 1950s and 1960s created new estates at King's Lynn, – and new schools. Here pupils of North Lynn Primary School (now St Edmund's) meet their new teachers in September 1953.

The Hunstanton Secondary Modern School created a huge stir among the world's architects when it opened in 1955, just before this picture was taken. Its innovative 'glasshouse' design has led to it being declared a listed building. All parts of the building were to be glazed with clear glass until, so local legend has it, someone remembered the need for changing-rooms...

A bay of three swings at Hayes Lane Playing Field, Fakenham, given by Mr F.S.Wigg, former chairman of the Parish Council, and Major and Mrs Ted Winser, together with their patrons at the Red Lion in August 1953.

Watts Naval School, North Elmham. Edmund Watts, of London, bought the school in 1901 and presented it to Dr Barnardo "for his orphans and destitute waifs". It accommodated 300 boys and the necessary staff but in 1949, under a regrouping scheme, many of the boys who wished to continue their training for a nautical career were transferred to Parkstone, Dorset. The school finally closed in December 1953.

Harvesting the Sea

The natural riches of the sea around Norfolk have attracted fishermen throughout the ages. But a combination of many factors such as changes in ecology, dwindling stocks and the vagaries of politics have all contributed to the decline of much of the fishing fleet. The days of the quayside of Yarmouth covered with the port's unique 'swills' (baskets) brim-full with herring are a thing of the past. But in spite of all the problems, many hundreds of people still make a living from the sea. Despite these days of hi-tech, fishing will always be a hard, unpredictable and sometimes dangerous way to make a living. This selection salutes those fishermen.

The *Golden Gain* from Fraserburgh and *Boy James* from Peterhead join other vessels moored four abreast at Yarmouth's South Quay in July 1970. Notice also the trucks on the railway line which ran along the quay.

The Fishwharf was a hive of activity when the Yarmouth and Scottish drifters brought in their large catches of herrings.

Scots boat *Sunlight* from Peterhead unloads its catch on to Yarmouth Fishwharf after successfully fishing the East Anglian Herring Voyage route.

Bob Davies (centre) assisted by his wife and Mr N.Everett, cleaning and cooking the morning's crab catch in May 1959. The firm is still trading in Cromer.

One of the many boats built by the Worfolk Brothers of King's Lynn was the yawl *Edward VII*, seen here being pushed away from the town's Fisher Fleet on 6 March 1974, when she was already 60 years old.

Herring drifters leaving Yarmouth to head for the fishing grounds.

By the time this photograph and others were taken by the *EDP* in February 1958, King's Lynn's ancient North End community was only a few years away from extinction by demolition and redevelopment. Here William Goodson, 88, is pictured with his nephews William James Benefer, 70, and Joseph Henry Goodson, 71 – retired fishermen all.

One of the unwelcome 'harvests' of the rich Wash shellfish beds is the occasional discovery of jettisoned bombs, and World War Two mines were being caught in fishing nets as late as the 1970s. A 1961 bomb disposal crew carefully prepares an area around a device before building a small wall of sandbags and setting off a controlled explosion.

Streets of Change

Although war has played its part in shaping Norfolk's towns, it was the redevelopment of the 1960s which had by far the biggest impact. In two towns, King's Lynn and Thetford, overspill agreements with the old London County Council sparked the building of massive new estates – and also led to the razing of old streets to make way for new shopping centres. Alongside this process, the disappearance of old-established family businesses under the onslaught of chain stores, pension funds and building societies has proceeded apace to this day.

Palmer Brothers shop and arcade, Yarmouth, in 1909. It was opened by Garwood Burton Palmer in June 1837, the year Princess Victoria became Queen. Notice the horse-drawn advertising boards and the roadsweeper's barrow, just visible in the bottom right-hand corner of this picture.

Fakenham Market Place from the tower of Ss Peter and Paul Church in May 1960. Part of Sheringham & Overman's office, behind the war memorial, has since been demolished to make way for FW Woolworth's store. Notice the people studying photographs in the window of the *Eastern Daily Press* office at the top left of the picture.

These shoppers seem oblivious to the car behind them in King's Lynn High Street in this picture taken during the early 1960s, years before pedestrianisation.

Part of the argument for levelling the North End homes of King's Lynn's seafaring community was the poor living
conditions endured by many people. This 1958 picture of a now-demolished home shows the most basic of kitchen
facilities. And note the dolly tub on the left of the picture; no washing machine here.

Fashion doesn't just turn full circle in clothes, it happens in shop design too. One of West Norfolk's best-loved shops was WH Smith in High Street, King's Lynn, as pictured here in 1957. Its elegant façade, moulded ceilings and wood panelling disappeared into the more utilitarian look of the supermarket chain next door when it took over the site in the 1970s. But, ironically, Laura Ashley was soon opening in the same Lynn street with a new look: elegant façade, wood panelling...

Under construction at Thetford in April 1969, the 1,000-house Abbey Farm estate, built to accommodate the overspill from London. The first people in the town expansion scheme had arrived ten years earlier. When completed the scheme had increased Thetford's population from 4,500 to nearly 13,000.

Campaigners watch as the new footbridge spanning the main Norwich-London road at Thetford is lowered into position in April 1971. Notice the children with their chopper bikes; nowadays they would probably all have mountain bikes. The lad on the left is making sure he is first across the bridge.

Thorpe Narrows by the King's Head public house, pictured here in June 1956, provided a bottleneck on the Norwich-Yarmouth road. A scheme was drawn up to widen 1,400 feet of the road. Fifteen houses had to be demolished, including these at the bottom of School Lane.

This unusual milestone, surmounted by a pineapple, stands at the junction of Holt High Street and Letheringsett Hill. It shows Lynn Regis (King's Lynn) as 34 miles away and Norwich as 21 miles.

Wells Road Post Office, Fakenham, where you could also buy Birds Eye foods, Brooke Bond tea and Lyons Maid ice-cream. The post-box is still mounted in the wall even though the building has been replaced.

King's Lynn is typical of many small towns in Norfolk and elsewhere which have seen the small shops and pubs which once crowded its main shopping streets largely supplanted by pension fund-owned sites taken by national stores or building societies. The change was well under way by the time this 1963 picture was taken in the High Street. Lynn's first supermarket, Elmo Food Fair, had opened in nearby Norfolk Street three years earlier; by 1971 the last over-the-counter grocer in High Street, David Greig, was announcing its closure.

Mail is loaded on to the horse-drawn Post Office van outside the Thetford office in this early, but undated scene. Another horse and cart makes its way past St Cuthbert's Church while a man reclines against the horse trough by the Market Place.

Autumn, a time for reflection... and this 1963 study perfectly captures the charm of St James' Park at King's Lynn. In the background are the now-demolished properties of St James' Road, cleared to make way for a car-park and the town's swimming pool.

Ss Peter and Paul's Church at Swaffham, seen here in 1962, has always been a favoured quiet spot for shoppers wishing to escape from the business of the town's market place a stone's throw away, especially when its famous Saturday market is in full swing. An indication too, that never-ending sales are not a recent phenomenon; the shop promises its sale will end on Friday 27 July, but the picture was taken on 13 August!

Messrs E.Bone's shop in Norwich Street, Fakenham, in March 1961. It was demolished with part of Fakenham Hardware next door to become the new home of the Co-operative Society.

The breadth of 1960s redevelopment can be seen in this 1961 view of New Conduit Street at King's Lynn. By the time the developers had finished, just three buildings (the solicitors' offices extreme left, the Post Office back centre and Hilton's shoes in the foreground) survived. One of the saddest losses was a seventeenth-century building associated with the family of George Vancouver, Lynn's famous explorer.

One seemingly irreversible trend in Norfolk life has been the closure of hundreds of the county's pubs over the years. Few could have had such a delightful name as The Tumbledown Dick, whose licensees Mr and Mrs Albert Trower of Pott Row, closed for good on 19 September 1965.

Wroxham Road, Sprowston, in October 1961 before it was widened. Many of the trees were later chopped down and the gardens shortened. There was considerable opposition in the parish to the widening scheme.

Men and women stand mardling in the Market Square at Aylsham in September 1963, while the local bus waits for more passengers. Notice the chemist's shop of G.R.Oke MPS and the International Stores. Ford, Austin and Morris have almost taken over the motor market!

The Friars, pictured south of the main London Road running across the picture, escaped the fate of much of King's Lynn's nineteenth-century heritage, which was swept away in the drive for urban regeneration in the 1960s. In the top left section of this 1959 view the former town hospital can be seen.

An evocative image of the 1960s demolition undergone by King's Lynn and other Norfolk towns. This picture was taken on 7 March 1968 as the old Union Street was bulldozed. In the background is the ancient All Saints' Church which alone survives from this scene, now surrounded by the 1960s flats complex of Hillington Square.

Before and After Beeching

The opening of the first railway line in Norfolk on 30 April 1844, between Norwich and Yarmouth, ushered in a revolution in communications. Rail links brought prosperity to moribund towns, decline to smaller ports, mass tourism to our coast and a decline in wherry and turnpike. But the invention of the car and better roads led to an inevitable decline in the numerous branch lines around Norfolk. The impact of the Beeching Report merely hastened the process. This section is a poignant look at the years of rail.

It is 1949 and the so-called 'Crab and Winkle' train leaves Swaffham station in a picture taken to mark the station's centenary. The station linked Swaffham with King's Lynn, Dereham, and Thetford at one stage. But the last train ran in 1963, ending the rail era for the town after 116 years (the first train had arrived in 1847, two years before the station was opened).

Branch line station staff often lavished tremendous care upon their railway station gardens. Here staff at Wolferton, on the Lynn-Hunstanton line, are pictured on 14 August 1953 with some of their prize-winning flower beds.

End of the line... The Lynn-Hunstanton line closed for good on 3 May 1969. The *EDP* was there to capture the historic moment for posterity. Driver Eddie Ashton (right) poses by the train. The wreath on the front of the train was placed by Mr L.W.Cogar of South Wootton.

Hemsby station on the old Midland and Great Northern line in May 1951. After closure it became an eyesore on the village's approach road.

After closure Thetford's railway station was put to good use as a youth hostel seen here in April 1965. It had the distinction of being the only hostel in the country to be housed in a railway station.

The 'Crewe of North Norfolk' was how Melton Constable was known because of its railway wagon sheet works, engineering shops, goods yards and engine sheds. Ninety-eight houses, some shown here in Melton Street in May 1963, were offered for sale to Walsingham Rural District Council by the Railway Authority after the workshops were closed. The offer was turned down and the houses were later bought by Norwich solicitor Mr Peter Tacon.

The derelict railway station at Massingham in November 1969 after the railway lines had been removed. The 18 miles of track between Rudham and King's Lynn, on the old Midland and Great Northern line, were being taken up by contractors to British Rail.

Aylsham North station looks a forlorn sight with the water and weeds in the old track bed.

We are Sailing...

Pleasure cruises are a speciality of the Broads and the East Norfolk resorts, and this selection of photographs is a chance to wallow in some pure nostalgia.

The *SS Resolute*, carrying four bands and jazz fans, leaves Yarmouth for Norwich on the outward half of the journey for a Sunday Riverboat Shuffle organised by the Bungay Jazz Club in June 1958.

The Yarmouth pleasure craft *Eastern Princess*, carrying holidaymakers on one of the last sea trips of the season in September 1962, passes drifter-trawlers preparing for the home fishing. Across the river are the premises of Watney Combe Reid & Co. Ltd.

The *Southtown* passes a well-laden ship bringing timber to Jewson's yard at Yarmouth in August 1961. The pleasure boat offered afternoon trips to Reedham, with an hour ashore, or whole-day trips to Wroxham on Mondays, Wednesdays and Thursdays. The two lads at the rail near the funnel look like twins.

Holidaymakers disembark from the *Janet* after a sea trip to Scroby Island off Great Yarmouth in July 1967.

The 1889 *Queen of the Broads* carrying passengers on a nine-hours-long Whit Sunday Broadland Jazz Shuffle. The event, recorded by the BBC in June 1957, featured three of East Anglia's leading bands – the Collegians, the Dixielanders and the Tailgate Jazz Band.

The Yarmouth pleasure steamer *Hotspur* sails from Britannia Pier carrying Army Cadets as part of a combined invasion exercise. Many of the cadets are wearing camouflaged steel helmets. Notice the Army officers on the bridge.

The 265-passenger *Yarmouth* approaches Gorleston in her river-trip days. Built in 1895 by Thomas Bradley and equipped with a Crabtree coal-fired engine, she served as a Royal Navy tender at Scapa Flow in World War One. She was put on display at St Katharine's-by-the-Tower, London, in 1973.

The *Norwich Belle* and *Eastern Princess* pleasure craft which operated from Hall Quay at Yarmouth, pictured in May 1961.

A pleasure boat with a difference photographed in July 1972. *Bubbly Jane* was renovated as a steamboat by her 25-year-old owner, Mr Rupert Latham, who also owned the Ernest Collins boatyard. He bought the hull for £75, removed its petrol engine and installed a steam engine, which was later replaced by another 70 to 100 years old.

The wherry *Dragon* sails away from the start leaving the handicapped *Albion* and *Hathor* still waiting for their starting signals in August 1952. The wherry race across Breydon Water began and finished at Burgh Castle Yacht Station.

In midstream the pleasure steamer *Yarmouth*, but loading at the quayside is the *Cobholm*. There does not appear to be much room aboard for the people queueing or buying tickets on this busy day in May 1976. Notice Cook's fresh fruit barrow beside the booking office.
The barges *Larch* and *Silver Birch* are moored across the river.

Sail was still an occasional visitor to King's Lynn in this 1966 view of the Purfleet. The *Will Everard* was one of the oldest sailing barges, with auxiliary engine, to use the East Coast ports. Alongside her is the now-demolished King's Staithe Square grain silos which had an unexpected role as background scenery (with suitable cladding) in the 1985 film *Revolution*.

For Those in Peril

If there was ever a perfect expression of the bravery of the lifeboat crews which man the county's coastline, then it is summed up in the Caister crew's motto "Never Turn Back". Norfolk's miles of sometimes treacherous sands have claimed many victims over the centuries, but also inspired outstanding acts of courage, exemplified in the story of Cromer's much-decorated Henry Blogg. Despite the vigilance of coastguard, lighthouse and lightship crews and lifeboatmen, tragedies still happen, a reminder of the fact that the North Sea is, at best, an uneasy ally for man.

Happisburgh High lighthouse, photographed here in April 1970, was powered by candles when it was built in 1791. When the familiar red and white bands were painted in 1883 an occulting light was installed, and in 1942 the light became powered by electricity. A Private Bill through Parliament in 1989 gave Happisburgh Light House Trust the status of a private lighthouse authority, thus ensuring the continuation of this boon to seafarers.

Station Officer A.McMaster (right) and Coastguard E.Stanley settling into their new look-out post at the top of a building overlooking Cromer promenade. Station Officer McMaster was communicating with Cromer No.1 lifeboat, which was on exercise in November 1953.

The plaster covering of the tower to Cromer lighthouse was being replaced by a cement coating in November 1952. In 1958 the light tower above the balustrade was replaced.

Cromer's No.2 lifeboat *Harriot Dixon* being brought in after returning from trials. The lifeboat had been overhauled and a new two-way radio set had been installed.

The strain increases, a line breaks so members of the Mundesley Coastguard Rescue Equipment Company prepare to put another line on board in a bid to prevent the Dutch coaster *Jonet* from swinging disastrously. The vessel, carrying 250 tons of bagged fertiliser, beached at Mundesley in thick fog in March 1969, but hit a groyne, demolishing the marker at its seaward end.

The Haisbro lightship being brought to port by the Yarmouth tug *Richard Lee Barber*. The lightship had been holed on her starboard side during a collision in February 1961.

The *Corncrake* ashore at Horsey Gap in December 1948. It must have been a schoolboy's dream fulfilled to be so close to a seagoing vessel.

Winterton Rocket Life Saving Company rescue some of the crew from the French trawler *St Pierre Eglise* which ran aground at Waxham in February 1955. Rocket lifesaving equipment was invented by Norfolkman Captain George William Manby (1765-1854).

The new Fowler Challenger submersible tractor under trials in April 1954 before being used to launch the Wells lifeboat.

Former Wells fishing boat *Viking of Wells* arrives at Caister Lifeboat Station after her six-and-a-half hour journey round the coast in April 1973. Four years after the Royal National Lifeboat Institution closed the Caister station Caister Volunteer Rescue Service bought the vessel for £4,500 and renamed her *Shirley Jean Adye*. Prior to fishing, the ex-RNLI Liverpool type twin-screw craft had served at St Abbs, Berwickshire, from 1953 to 1964.

The 183-ton Lynn
Well lightship LV89
berthed at Norwich
in August 1974.
Cringleford potato
merchant Mr
Dennis Smith had
bought her for
£7,500 and let the
Sea Cadets use her
for training
purposes.

Almost the length of the port side of the Lowestoft trawler *Kastor* washed ashore on Caister North beach in
May 1969. Wreckage from the vessel was found from Caister to north of Lowestoft.

Days of Drama

This section looks at some of the dramatic incidents the *Eastern Daily Press* has covered over the years.

A Trident airliner which crashed at Felthorpe, killing its test crew of four. G-ARPY, which was due to be handed over to British European Airways, crashed into a field next to the airstrip used by Felthorpe Flying Group in June 1966.

A fireman damps down the smoking remains of the sports pavilion at the West Norfolk Recreation Ground, King's Lynn, which was gutted by fire in March 1972.

Firemen using a turntable escape trying to save the north-east corner of Old Buckenham Hall which was being gutted by fire in December 1952.

With so many air bases around Norfolk (by the end of the war there were no fewer than 37 airfields), crashes were, sadly, a fairly common occurrence. This previously unpublished picture shows the aftermath of one such crash, at Bexwell near Downham Market on 18 July 1952. A Harvard trainer aircraft from RAF Feltwell crashed into a field of oats on Mr G.W.Martin's Church Farm, killing the pilot.

In June 1976 a ball of fire and a mushroom cloud of choking white-grey fumes followed the explosion at Dow Chemical, King's Lynn, which killed one worker and could be heard 17 miles away at Hunstanton. Fifty firemen, manning ten appliances and backed by three ambulances, rushed to the complex and police quickly evacuated the area. The blast was in drying equipment in a plant which manufactured poultry feed additive.

A section of a plane lies smouldering in potato field after a Canberra bomber from Germany collided with a Victor tanker from RAF Marham over Holt in August 1968. Seven RAF officers died in the crash.

The remains of Broom Boats Ltd *Wave Chief I* lie submerged or scattered on the bank near Reedham after being sliced in two by the coaster *Union Moon* in July 1978. Whilst travelling downstream from Norwich the coaster's steering gear failed; the master went hard astern and gave warning blasts on his siren before hitting the craft bow first. The families, who were having lunch on board the moored cruiser, managed to open a window and throw one of their children on to the bank before scrambling out unhurt.

This plaque in Acle fire station is a reminder of the three-day bunker blaze which was one of the worst fires in living memory. Sixty feet below ground firemen had battled through a maze of tunnels choked with acrid smoke and flames. "Hell in the Hole" was the nickname RAF personnel gave to the underground building. A leading aircraftman was later charged with unlawfully and maliciously setting fire to an installation within the confines of the RAF station at Neatishead.

All Friends Together

It is said that wherever three Englishmen gather, one will become a club chairman, one a treasurer and one the secretary. Norfolk too has its diverse selection of clubs and societies, ranging from brass bands to Scouts. This photographic section has a nostalgic look at some of them.

The ceremonial parade of standards (including those of Girl Scouts of America based in the county) at the Norfolk Girl Guides Jubilee Rally held at Norwich Training College, Keswick, in July 1960. Five thousand Girl Guides, Rangers, Cadets and Brownies attended the eight-hour rally, and the parade was directed by Miss Mollie Coleman.

Olave, Lady Baden-Powell, the World Chief Guide, places the Medal of Merit on Miss Mollie Coleman, Division Secretary for Norwich and County Song Leader, at the Norfolk Girl Guides' Jubilee Rally at Norwich Training College, Keswick, in July 1960. Standing behind Lady Baden-Powell is the Hon Beryl Cozens-Hardy.

Queen Mary attends a Girl Guides ceremony at Great Massingham in 1923.

Cromer and Sheringham Town band, 1967 champions of the East Anglian Brass Band Association. Behind the trophies are Mr Henry L.Bishop (band president) and Mr H.J.Grice (bandmaster). The treasurer and secretary, Mr C.D.L.Palmer, is fourth from left in the middle row.

Patrol Leaders Ronald C.Fiske and John Griffin receive their Scout Cords from Mr W.J.'Inky' England, Assistant County Commissioner for Training, at a meeting of the 1st North Walsham Boy Scout Troop in January 1953. The Scout Cords were the highest award for Scouts under the age of 15 years.

A 300-strong St John Ambulance Brigade parade drawn up at Watton County Secondary School after attending Watton Church. Ambulance and nursing members, together with cadets, from Attleborough, Dereham, East Harling, Hingham, Hockering, Lopham, Mattishall, Swaffham, Thetford, Watton, Wendling and Wymondham were listening to an address by their Commissioner-in-Chief (Lieutenant General Sir Otto Lund) in October 1953.

Blooming marvellous... The horticultural show has always been one of the mainstays of village and town life in Norfolk. In this 1967 picture, Mr Bill Paterson, chairman of Hunstanton UDC, and his wife admire exhibits in the Hunstanton and District Gardens and Allotments Association annual show. Also pictured are, from left, Colonel Graham Richmond, John Storey and Wing Commander R.Stuart Mudie.

The time: 17 May 1952, the place: Gaywood Park School, King's Lynn, and the occasion: two Land Rangers from the 1st Dersingham Company, including Mary Smith (right), present a silver pen and pencil set to Mrs Clifton-Brown to mark her appointment as County Commissioner for Norfolk, succeeding Lady Somerleyton. The Girl Guides were meeting as part of a rally for North West Norfolk members.

King's Lynn and Terrington post of the Royal Observer Corps photographed in practice during late 1952 or early 1953 in the old Army Drill Hall at Wellesley Street, Lynn.

Members of the 30th Norwich Troop putting up the gate which formed the entrance to their section of the Keswick Festival Rally. The rally, in May 1951, was attended by 1,000 Boy Scouts and 600 Girl Guides. The Chief Guide, Lady Baden-Powell, said it was the first time anywhere in the country that Scouts and Guides had held a joint camp.

Another use for a Scout trek-cart. Scouts from the 1st Diss Group delivering the first 40 parcels from the Rotary Club to the elderly and needy of the town in December 1963. Left to right: Michael Madgett, Stephen Cobb, Patrol Leader Stephen Wilby, Patrol Leader John Pitchers and Martin Lord.

Christmas is Coming

Christmas and nostalgia go hand-in-hand, of course. So enjoy wallowing in the tinsel and decorations of yesteryear – and marvel at the group of swimmers performing a very Norfolk, and very b-r-r-r-ave, Christmas tradition.

Getting the Christmas decorations right took on a special meaning at Wolferton station. Station staff prepare the station for the arrival of the royal family on one of their traditional Christmas and New Year holidays.

For unto us a child is born... pupils of All Saints' School at King's Lynn give a Bible reading as part of their 1968 Christmas service.

Aldiss' department store at Fakenham lit up for the Christmas season in November 1967.

Visiting Santa has always been a special part of that pre-Christmas build-up. Here, on 6 December 1961, Judith Hase (8) and her brother Patrick (3) discuss their Christmas list with the Father Christmas at Jermyn's department store, King's Lynn.

The choir of Taverham Hall School giving their triennial Ceremony of Carols to an audience of parents in December 1966.

The Christmas Day swim at Hunstanton has built up from a few hardy souls in the mid-1950s, to a mass fancy dress dip watched by crowds in the thousands every year. This 1970 picture shows Andrew Ramsay, Michael Watt and Tim Reynolds. Tim set a record for staying in – four minutes. The trio had to cross a snow-covered beach to reach the sea. He said "It really was surprisingly warm. I think we must be getting used to it."

This Sporting Life

Norfolk people have always loved their sport, although the days when five-figure crowds attended speedway and non-League football seem gone forever. Here is a sample of some of the sporting activities which have engaged Norfolk people over the years.

A rousing start to the Archie Scott-Brown Trophy race at Snetterton as historic racing cars leave the grid to make 20 laps of the circuit in September 1969.

Competitors at the sand pit during the fourth heat of the Hadler Trophy for 225 to 250cc machines at the Eastern Centre Scramble Championships held at Cadder's Hill, Lyng in August 1966.

It is 3 January 1957, and the West Norfolk Pony Club (led by its master Major Robert Hoare, centre), huntsmen and hounds gather before moving off from Middleton Tower just outside King's Lynn.

On the beat: the nine-strong women beaters group based at West Acre, pictured on 23 December 1964. The group was formed in 1953, and when this picture was taken the youngest member was Mrs Peggy Thaxton, aged 22. The group worked three days a week during the pheasant season on the Birkbeck estate.

Matches in Group 5 of the Men's Inter-County Tennis Championships under way at Cromer in July 1963. The tennis courts at Norwich Road were laid down in 1907. Among famous players to use the courts were Ann Haydon, who won Wimbledon in 1969, Lords Cholmondley, Roundway and Wolverhampton, and Sir Samuel Hoare, who later became Lord Templewood.

Yarmouth Bloaters Speedway team 1949-51. Back row (left to right): Billy Bales (the Tiny Tearaway), Stan Page, Johnny White, Bill Carruthers, Reg Morgan and Tip Mills. Front row: team captain Sid Hipperson (on bike) and Cliff Ladbrooke.

When the Norwich Stars speedway team shut up shop in the city in October 1964, promoters Maurice Littlechild and Jack Thompson searched everywhere for an alternative site. They found it at the Saddlebow stadium at King's Lynn. The first meeting was held on 23 May 1965 in front of 6,300 fans. This 1969 picture shows a scene from the pits at a practice session.

Competitors in Norfolk County Rifle Association's annual outdoor pistol championships at Horsford range in June 1975.

The Dr Fisher Memorial Cricket Pavilion at the Lawn, Fakenham was opened in June 1957 by Mr Stuart Surridge, former captain of Surrey County Cricket Club. A cricket bat was used to lay one of the foundation stones instead of the usual builder's trowel, and Fakenham Cricket Club's pavilion was built with the help of volunteers.

Young riders await their turn at Cringleford Gymkhana in September 1968.

One corner of the Walks park at King's Lynn is taken up by the stadium of Lynn FC, known as the Linnets. But the nature of the topography gives a chance for a passing walker to enjoy a view of the game. As the photographer wrote in this 1953 picture "Not everyone goes through the turnstiles and the quality of the entertainment varies."

Enthusiasms

A short section showing some of the ways Norfolk people have turned their hobby into expressions of beauty and engineering skill.

Graham Fulcher, of Honington, at the East Anglian Traction Engine Club rally in Euston Park in July 1967. The Hoverbat, which had three 250cc engines, travelled on a cushion of air and was one of only 30 in the country.

Mr T.Wood (right) with his home-made model of a Burrell traction engine during the Bysteam Rally held at Bawburgh in August 1975.

Glandford Shell Museum, photographed here in August 1975, was built in 1915 by the late Sir Alfred Jodrell, Bart., of Bayfield Hall. It was to house a collection of shells which he had made over a period of 60 years.

Mrs J.A.Johnston (left), of White Cottage, Worstead, talks to her weaving class in the village in March 1950.

Mrs Elizabeth Smith, of Briston, and her daughter, Christine, with some of her corn dollies in December 1973. A member of the Norfolk Rural Craftsman's Guild, she had a 'repertoire' of 80 different shapes. One featuring a decorated horse's head was sent to Princess Anne and Captain Mark Phillips as a wedding gift.

Testing the bells at St Nicholas' Chapel, King's Lynn, is not an occupation for the faint-hearted – or the delicate of hearing, as can probably be guessed at by the fingers inserted firmly in the ears of the bellringer. Of course, the photographer was not quite so lucky...!

What started as a hobby for Mrs Mary-Anne Matts, pictured here in August 1973, became a busy cottage craft at Aldborough.

In the Footsteps of History

Norfolk's past has an important role in shaping the county's present. From its huge selection of medieval churches to castles, much remains of the historic legacy of the people who have changed Norfolk's history. Many of the sites pictured in this section have unexpected stories of their own, such as the location of North Norfolk's first hotel – centuries before 'Poppyland' – and how James Bond's creator got involved in the search for buried treasure...

Figure heads, photographed in August 1955. Said to represent the four seasons of the year, ornament the porch of a 300-year-old cottage at Burnham Overy.

Partially hidden by the tall Thornbury Tower is
the Chapel built at Costessey Hall by Sir William
Jerningham in 1809. In the background is the
wooded area known as 'The Wilderness' which
extended to the Norwich-Dereham road. Tradition
has it that the ghost of the Lady in Green would
haunt the contractors for the rest of their lives if
the Thornbury Tower was fully demolished. The
contents were sold by auction in December 1913
and most of the hall was demolished in the 1920s
and 1930s.

The whipping post under
the Market Cross at New
Buckenham pictured here
in August 1962.

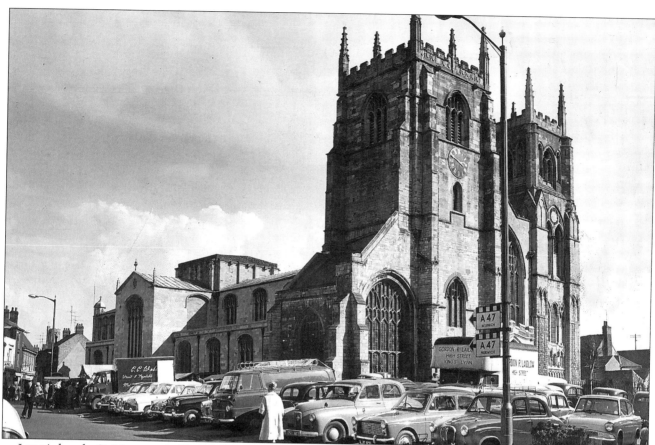

Lynn's lovely St Margaret's Church has survived storm, earthquake, flood and bombardment by Cromwell's troops in its eventful 800-year history. Now it serves as the backdrop for the town's Saturday market, and for the rest of the week the market place is turned over to cars, as in this 1962 view.

Tradition has it that the monks of North Creake Abbey buried a great cache of gold and silver to prevent it from falling into the hands of King Henry VIII's assessors. In June 1953 author Ian Fleming and a three-man team from the Royal Engineers with an electronic mine-detector spent three days trying to find it. They were unsuccessful!

The Bishop of Norwich (Dr Launcelot Fleming) preaches during the service for Broads holidaymakers at St Benet's Abbey in August 1964. Whilst the choristers sit on the grass and some of the clergy recline on the farm trailer the gowned accompanist sits at the harmonium. Amplification for the service was provided by Yaxleys of Norwich.

Reedham stonemason Mr Derek Pond renovating Hardley Cross in April 1971. This boundary of the Yare waters within which the citizens of Norwich hold rights and liberties was defined by a charter in 1556.

Originally erected in the middle of the sixteenth century by Thomas Thirlby, Bishop of Norwich, North Walsham's Market Cross suffered considerable damage in the town fire of June 1600. This picture was taken in the days of trust when bicycles could be left unlocked. Notice the 1725 fire pump which used to be on show under the cross.

The twelfth-century church at Thorpe St Andrew was demolished about 1882, leaving only the square tower and south wall. In this picture the windows are boarded up, and behind the thatched roof can be seen the present day church built in 1866.

Founder's Day at Trinity Hospital, Castle Rising, in February 1957. The residents, in their capes and tall hats, watch the joint of meat being cooked before the open fire. Henry Howard, Earl of Northampton, had the building constructed between 1609 and 1615. According to the statutes the women who live there 'must be no common beggar, harlot, scold, drunkard, haunter of taverns, inns and alehouses'.

Cavell House, Swardeston Common, in January 1940 – the birthplace of nurse Edith Cavell. She was executed by an eight-man firing squad at 7am on the 12 October 1915 for running a secret escape route from Belgium for Allied Soldiers. In just under ten months she had saved the lives of 200 men.

The Franciscan Friary at Little Walsingham, pictured here in January 1936, was founded by the Greyfriars in 1347.

The folly tower at Pine Banks, Thorpe St Andrew, was built by John Taylor, solicitor, in the late 1870s. From it one could see the coastline from Sheringham in North Norfolk to Southwold in East Suffolk.

Wymondham's Market Cross, pictured here in October 1970, was built in 1618 to replace a timber cross destroyed by fire three years earlier. It contains a half-timbered octagonal room supported on eight pillars. One could say the under part doubled as a bus shelter for the bus stop alongside!

Castle Acre's twelfth-century priory was used by the Cluniac order. In 1351 King Edward III ordered the arrest of the monks who had become 'vagabonds in England in secular habit.' Since the Commissioners of HM Works were appointed guardians in 1929 a great deal had been done in cleaning, excavating and restoring by the time this 1957 view was taken.

Greyfriars Tower at King's Lynn has been a landmark for ships since medieval times. It is now the centrepiece for the municipal Tower Gardens which are a favoured peaceful haunt of shoppers and office workers alike. In this picture, taken on 5 May 1952, visitors admire the tulip displays.

Yarmouth Fishermen's Hospital after modernisation – each self-contained residence had been given its own separate kitchen, bathroom and lavatory. Mr E.Rant is seen here putting the finishing touches to the sandstone carved fishing smack which he had repainted in December 1961. St Peter looks on from the cupola.

The Slipper Chapel at Houghton St Giles was built about 1350. It was here that Henry VIII and many other pilgrims are said to have removed their shoes before walking barefoot to the Shrine of Our Lady in Walsingham. The chapel was given to the Roman Catholic Church by Miss Charlotte Boyd in 1897. Since this picture was taken in July 1927 the Holy Ghost Chapel has been built to the left and a priest's house to the right. Notice the pump between the wall and the chapel window.

The former Benedictine Priory at Horsham St Faith was founded between 1100 and 1135. About 1536 the refectory was converted into a private house, and it was here in 1561 that the future martyr and saint, Robert Southwell, was born. He was hanged and beheaded at Tyburn in 1595. The house contains the finest examples of thirteenth-century refectory wall paintings to be found in England.

A man stands contemplating the ruins of the 'Saxon Cathedral' at North Elmham. In the background is the church of St Mary the Virgin. Elmham was a bishopric from AD 673 to 870.

Workmen of the Ministry of Works busy in the ruins of Thetford's twelfth-century Cluniac priory. They were laying sand on the old floor tiles in September 1959 to prevent frost damage during the coming winter.

The Market Cross at New Buckenham, pictured here in May 1958, was possibly built as a shop in the mid-sixteenth century, but converted to its present form at the beginning of the eighteenth century. The carved panel between the two sets of windows shows Buckenham Castle, and is thought to be late-fifteenth century.

Wymondham's Benedictine Priory was built between the twelfth and fifteenth centuries and became an abbey in 1449. At the Dissolution the abbey was pulled down and the Norman nave became the parish church, pictured here in July 1976.

St James' Church at Bawsey, better known as Bawsey Ruins, is one of the most evocative deserted medieval sites in Norfolk, perched on a hill overlooking the busy A149. This 1952 picture shows Ernie Shipp, Edward Greenacre, Robert Greenacre and Charles Tovell ringing handbells during a harvest thanksgiving.

Beeston Priory, near Sheringham, was founded by the Augustinians in the twelfth century. Because of its position halfway between the two major ports of Cromer and Blakeney the prior and his canons offered refuge for travellers in the thirteenth century – thereby becoming North Norfolk's first hoteliers.

That's Entertainment

"We had to make our own entertainment..." our grandparents' constant refrain is alive and kicking in Norfolk. From thriving amateur dramatic societies to horticultural clubs, thousands of people in Norfolk's 750-plus towns and villages are busy putting on shows, village fêtes, arranging talks or just organising a chance for people to have a cup of tea and a good 'mardle'. This section is dedicated to that stalwart band of organisers. And there's a little reminder for anyone who was ever a 'Minor of ABC'.

The Collegians play a session at a Broadland Jazz Shuffle on the *Queen of the Broads* pleasure steamer in June 1957.

The cast of summer show *Secombe Here* arrives for rehearsal at Yarmouth's Wellington Pier in May 1962. In the centre, with hat and glasses, is the star – Harry Secombe. Others in the cast included Ronnie Corbett, Dennis Spicer with Monkey Doll, Ted Carson, Audrey Jeans and Stephanie Voss.

Billy Matchett, the 74-year-old chairman of the Old Time Music Hall at Gorleston Pavilion, batting in the Variety Artistes' Charity Cricket Match at Wellesley Recreation Ground, Great Yarmouth, in August 1964. Captains of the two teams, comprised of artistes from the local shows, were Eric Morecambe and Ernie Wise.

Crowds of civic dignitaries from all over East Anglia gather at the opening of the Lynn Mart in 1970, a scene repeated around every St Valentine's Day for generations. This scene has been a popular one for photographers since Victorian times, and Mart postcards are much sought after by local collectors and those interested in fairground memorabilia.

Lynn Mart, held every February, has always held a special place in showmen's hearts as the first date in their calendar. This unusual 1970 view was taken from the top of the helter skelter and shows some of the stalls and rides packed into Tuesday Market Place. Attractions change each year; 1970 saw the popular Jets ride (left) where your shilling bought you the thrill of 'controlling your own plane'.

Don't be shy... the village fête remains as popular a part of Norfolk life as it ever was. Here, at Heacham's 1968 summer fête, a youngster is all concentration as he lets fly at a coconut.

Waiters prepare their trays for the annual Waiters' Race at Cromer in August 1963. As every tray has a bottle of Martini on it one presumes they must have sponsored the race.

'We're all friends together, we are the Minors of ABC!' went the refrain at the Majestic Cinema, King's Lynn when the Saturday morning 'flicks' enjoyed a huge popularity. These ABC members are seen receiving their prizes in a Guy Fawkes competition on 2 November 1968. Showing at the Majestic were Elvis Presley's *Tickle Me* supported by *The Count of Monte Cristo*. And among the attractions at the ABC Minors club was that hardy perennial, *Flash Gordon*.

Floats from the Friendship Club and St John Ambulance Brigade take part in a Cromer Carnival procession in the 1

Whilst bowls teams from Norwich and Yarmouth Corporations battle it out on the rinks in July 1951, whistler/yodeller Ronnie Ronalde and Max Bygraves were entertaining audiences at the Britannia Pier. In addition to ice cream and tea, Horlicks was also available at the tea stalls.

Ex-ter-min-ate! King's Lynn Operatic and Dramatic Society brought in a topical 'guest star' for their 1965 pantomime *Mother Goose*... a replica of Dr Who's Daleks, built and operated by Ralph Melton. A snowy Walks at Lynn was the backdrop for this picture to tie in with the show.

Crafts of the Countryside

Watching a country craftsman at work is to watch man in perfect balance with his environment. The taking of a few willow twigs, for example, to weave them into a thing of utility and beauty is something still appreciated in these days of mass production and uniformity. Sadly, some of the crafts shown here have all but vanished from the Norfolk scene.

Right: Charles O'Connor pushed his hand-cart knife-grinding machine from town to town as he travelled the British Isles. By April 1961, when this photograph was taken, he had mounted it on the back of a lorry and continued calling house-to-house sharpening anything from knives to lawnmowers.

Apprentice Will Cowling, son of George, cutting house tiles into correct lengths at Barney brickworks in November 1952. The tiles were then shaped and had their corners cut off by Mr Albert Burton.

George Cowling turns out bricks from their moulds at Barney brickworks in November 1952.

Making linen pegs from ash wood was one of the pastimes of 73-year-old John Harris, of the Common, Whissonsett seen here in October 1953. He was known to his intimates as 'Old Cardy'.

Reed cutting on Barton Broad in February 1939.

Contrasting methods of transportation in a Norfolk rural industry are demonstrated in the unloading and loading of reeds at Thurne Dyke in March 1967.

Thatching the Tudor
building with Norfolk
reed at Mergate Farm,
Bracon Ash in July 1967.

Mr Joseph Smalls, 84-
year-old basket maker of
North Creake, at work
on a straw armchair.

Mr R.Townshend, chairmaker, marking up wood for sawing in October 1950.

Plaiting rushes at Wheatacre in March 1947.

One of the most ancient trades in the land – charcoal burning. Mr E.Humphrey and Mr McMahon are seen bagging up the charcoal after 'cooking' logs in kilns at Thorpe Market in December 1955.

Seventy-year-old Mr Albert E.Wymer of Hevingham, making a besom birch broom in April 1960. Once he had prepared the materials he could produce a dozen brooms every 90 minutes.

Riven oak pales being made at Farman's workshops at North Walsham in June 1953. Mr Farman is holding a completed gate.

Mr J.G.Rix, harness maker of Acle, at work in May 1951.

Molten metal being guided into moulds to form parts for pumping machinery and electrical equipment. This foundry was at Walsingham.

Foreman basket maker Mr Fred Nettleship seen here in May 1955 working on a 'sow' (shop on wheels), one of the wide variety of articles made at the wholesale basket and cane furniture shop of Stanley Bird Basketware Ltd of Friar's Lane, Great Yarmouth.

A new rural industry pictured in January 1951 – making straw packings for protecting wine and other bottles in transit was started by Strawpacks Ltd of Glandford, near Holt. The machines formed a rough cylinder of straw which then went to another machine for finishing. Notice the absence of guards on the machines.

Left: Mr. George Wharton, of Briton Brush Co. Ltd, Wymondham, is busy at his bench making a bass broom in November 1949. Even in the days of mass production the pride of the craftsman remained in some jobs. *Right:* Hazel and willow fencing made by the North Walsham firm of W.R.Farman Ltd being loaded on to a lorry in October 1960 for eventual shipment to New York.

Boxer the Percheron stands with Mr W.Beckett at the doorway of Hempnall smithy in March 1955. Getting the new shoe ready at the forge is Mr C.Taylor, who is watched by Mr S.J.Watts.

Boatbuilding

A brief look at some of the boat-building traditions in the county, servicing both sea-going needs and the vast Broads network of inland waterways.

New motor cruisers under construction at Messrs Graham Bunn's workshop at Wroxham in March 1954. They were for delivery to a hire fleet, replacing craft which had been in service for six or seven years.

A rare 1957 view of the Worfolks' boatyard in the Friars, King's Lynn. The picture shows (from left) Vic Pratt – now a ships' chandler – George Walker and Johnny Drew. They are pictured building nine-foot dinghies for Tom Percival of Horning. Mr Pratt, who began as an apprentice in the yard in 1945, is still an expert boat builder – in 1995 his self-designed day boat won the Wooden Boat Show at Greenwich.

Manufacturing glass-fibre boats at Bunn's workshop, Wroxham, in January 1961.

Evinrude and Mercury outboard engines being serviced at Landamore's of Wroxham in March 1964 before the beginning of a new season.

Sailmakers putting their skills into practice at Jeckells of Wroxham in March 1964.

Yacht A855 being checked over at Herbert Woods' yard, Potter Heigham, in March 1963 before the start of the season.

Up, Down, Over and Sideways

The rather cryptic title of this section refers to the way in which the various bridges pictured in this section operate. Bridges are a vital part of the transport links of the county, which is almost surrounded on the land side by the Rivers Nene, Ouse, Little Ouse and Waveney – and that's not counting all the miles of Broads of course. In fact the link over the Ouse at King's Lynn was so important that Britain's biggest civil temporary bridge was constructed there to keep those vital links open. And the soldiers who built it cleaned up in a rather unexpected fashion...

This bridge, pictured in January 1971 and built in 1709 over the River Stiffkey at Houghton St Giles, is passed by thousands of pilgrims walking the Holy Mile from the Slipper Chapel to Walsingham.

A wooden bridge over the River Glaven at Glandford seen here in August 1948.

The new Haddiscoe Bridge towers above the old hand-operated two-leaf bascule, built in 1827 by the Norwich and Lowestoft Navigation Company, as a Broads cruiser passes along the New Cut in May 1961. In days gone by the toll was collected by the Bridgeman using an adapted butterfly net on a long stick into which the yachtsman would place the coin.

Two new counter-balanced ramps have been added to each end of the rebuilt Reedham ferry which greatly aid loading and unloading, and also act as a safety measure against overshooting. Notice-the Jowett Bradford van on board in this April 1952 photograph, but shame on them for flying the Union Flag upside-down.

It's just temporary... that's what the people of Downham West were told when the timber bridge on the right of this picture was built to replace the Victorian iron bridge spanning the Ouse. In the event they had to wait 27 years before a £75,000 replacement bridge finally superseded both structures. Lord Lieutenant of Norfolk, Sir Edmund Bacon, opened the structure in 1965. The aerial picture shows work in progress in November 1964.

The swing bridge which enabled the rail link across Breydon Water. Built at the beginning of the century, the whole structure was 626 feet in length and weighed more than 1,000 tons. The Yarmouth pleasure boat *Resolute* is passing through the open section.

The London coaster *Sedulity* passing the railway swingbridge at Reedham. When the bridge was opened in 1904 the 260-ton central span was moved by a motor and starter built by the Norwich firm Laurence Scott & Company a year earlier. The motor, still in working order, was replaced after 63 years of service.

When engineers discovered the ageing Cut Bridge at King's Lynn needed to be closed for reconstruction, it threatened huge disruption to the vital A47 trunk road. But then the 48th Field Sqn of the Yorkshire 39th Engineer Regiment stepped in to help. They built a 550-feet temporary bridge – the biggest temporary bridge for public use in Britain – in just six weeks. The bridge opened in December 1969 and was dismantled in January 1971. As a grateful thank you, the people of Lynn ran a fund for the soldiers. The money was, at the regiment's request, spent on new washing machines.

Flood!

No one who experienced the 1953 floods will ever forget them. For generations, Norfolk people had accepted the occasional inundation with a shrug of the shoulders; few made any attempt to move out of flood areas, because a flood disaster was something far-off and which might never happen.

But on 31 January 1953 it did. A combination of an exceptional high tide and freak storm conditions at sea produced an unstoppable surge which rendered man's existing sea defences virtually useless. By the end of that terrible night 105 people had lost their lives in the storm, 32 in one town alone (Hunstanton). If there was one silver lining to the tragedy it was that it brought out the very best in Norfolk people, with many astounding acts of bravery. And the enormous clean-up and repair operations revived memories of the wartime 'Dunkirk spirit'. We never underestimated the sea again.

There were no shortage of Prince Charmings willing to take stranded girls to dry land and safety. This picture was taken at King's Staithe Square, King's Lynn. The photographer could not resist adding wryly to his caption: 'The staff photographer who took this picture was in deeper water.'

London Road, King's Lynn, is one of the main thoroughfares into town. But on the night of the floods, shocked householders could do little but watch the floodwaters rise.

The flood waters rage at Sea Palling, destroying much of what stands in their path.

Cley windmill stands as a sentinel as flood waters lap at the surrounding buildings.

A stricken lorry lies trapped by floodwater as an ambulance crew hurries to a casualty at Snettisham.

Flood escapees sit together by candlelight in a King's Lynn house and ponder the night's horrors.

Leading fireman Fred Sadd helps with the rescue of a dog. On the night of the flood Fred, of the Gorleston sub-station, spent hours in the icy water pushing and pulling boatloads of trapped people to safety. Three months later he was awarded the George Medal for his bravery.

Horse-lover Arthur Benjafield rides one of the ponies rescued from the Cobholm area of Yarmouth. He had spent every available minute since the floods began in rescuing livestock from the smallholdings and allotments in the district.

Royal Canadian Air Force men helped in the rescue effort at Yarmouth, and one man insisted that his goldfish came too!

"Shucks, it wasn't much".
That was the modest
statement by 22-year-old
American serviceman Reis
Leming referring to his efforts
to rescue at least 27 people
stranded in storm-wrecked
Hunstanton beach bungalows.
Reis, seen here re-creating his
rescue action for the *EDP*, was
awarded the George Medal.
Forty years later, the *EDP*
arranged for Reis to be flown
back to Hunstanton for an
emotional return.

The coast road at Walcot is
littered with debris from
smashed cliff-top bungalows, and
shingle, sand and seaweed from
the beach.

Sand and rubbish was up to mantle-shelf height in most of the houses near the sea at Sea Palling. The occupants of this house were digging away to salvage what they could.

Families being evacuated at Salthouse, a village which suffered severely from the sea's encroachment.

Everything stops for tea… a welcome break for servicemen involved in the flood relief effort. Hunstanton Town Hall was the centre for this particular hospitality.

With homes wrecked by up to eight feet of flood water at South Lynn, emergency centres were set up, such as this one at South Lynn Baptist Church. Only a few hundred yards from the centre 15 people had perished.

Gaywood Park School at King's Lynn became a temporary centre for many of the displaced families from South Lynn. The Queen, the Duke of Edinburgh and the Duke of Gloucester visited to give their support to the flood victims.

A colossal task for the Eastern Electricity Board at Yarmouth – repairing and cleaning motors and other electrical equipment affected by the flooding. This was one of their workshops at Electric House in Regent Road.

Service personnel and civilians work together to seal a gap in the dunes at Sea Palling.

1953 was not the only flood of course... 11 January 1978, and driver Ron Fitzgerald never forgot the night he decided to take a short-cut through King's Lynn. Unluckily for him, he'd picked the same night as one of Lynn's worst-ever floods. Ron, of Thompson, near Watton, is seen here about to get stuck on the town's London Road, despite the advice of this passer-by.

The Miller's Tale

Time was when virtually every Norfolk village had its own water or windmill. They were so commonplace that a nineteenth-century guidebook once featured the North Norfolk village of Cley without a single mention of its beautiful windmill, which to modern eyes is its most important feature. Sadly, relatively few remain, although strenuous efforts have been made by private individuals and voluntary groups to restore and preserve what is left. This section is a look at some of the county's mills. Poignantly, some have succumbed to fire or demolition since the *EDP* pictured them.

Hunsett Old Mill on the River Ant is passed by a couple enjoying a day out on the Norfolk Broads.

The four-storey mill on the
River Bure at Buxton, pictured
here in March 1961, dates from
1754 and is scheduled as a
building of architectural or
historic interest. Duffields Mills
group closed the mill in 1970,
making ten of their staff
redundant. It later became an
arts centre with craft workshops,
an art gallery and restaurant, but
in January 1991 it was ravaged
by fire.

Restoration work to Burnham
Overy Staithe Mill being carried out
by Messrs R.Thompson & Son, of
Lincolnshire. A new balcony had
been fitted to the mill, but what
were six pairs of ladies' shoes doing
on the beam in the foreground?

Former London journalist and author Derek Neville walks his dogs near his unusual home at Itteringham in March 1961. The seventeenth-century watermill, which spans the River Bure, ceased working before World War One and fell into decay. In 1938 it was restored and converted into a dwelling house.

Looking for all the world like 'Deadwood Gulch', this view is in fact Denver Mill pond during that long hot summer in 1976. The 'skull' in the foreground is really an old branch.

The mill at Burgh-next-Aylsham pictured in March 1961. There is mention in the Domesday Book that a mill stood on this site.

Sprowston post mill, built in the early 1730s and commonly known as Crome's mill, was owned by members of the Harrison family. The mill was destroyed in March 1933 when flames from a small bonfire set light to gorse and furze. Wind carried the flames up the hill and within minutes the mill was burning.

Smoke still rises from Horstead Mill the morning after it was partly destroyed by fire in January 1963.

Agricultural Shows

The Royal Norfolk Show held at Costessey – but previously 'travelling' around several venues in the county – is *the* event of the year for thousands of people in the county. It is a perfect annual reminder of the importance agriculture still plays in the Norfolk economy – and the county's big day out. The show tradition is strong in Norfolk, and it is one where once again the royal connection is strong, both through official visits and the monarch's position as one of Norfolk's leading landowners.

Crowds of local people gather to enjoy the spectacle of the Royal Norfolk Show in July 1957.

King George VI, Queen Elizabeth and Princess Margaret are escorted by Sir Edmund Bacon on their visit to the 1950 show held at Anmer. Behind them is Captain S.H. Van Neck, Chief Constable of Norfolk Constabulary.

The Queen Mother's appearance at the annual July Sandringham Show is always a highlight of the West Norfolk calendar. On her 1956 visit to the show she admires some of the entrants to the rabbit class.

St George (eight-year-old Jackie Thrower of Yaxham) and the Dragon (her brother, David, aged 10) were winners of the fancy dress event at the Aylsham Show in September 1969.

Red Poll cattle are
paraded round the ring at
the 1955 show. Stands
and marquees bear the
names of the Ministry of
Agriculture, Calor Gas,
BOCM, Cannell's Seeds
and the West Norfolk
Farmers' Manure and
Chemical Co-operative
Co Ltd.

Mr E.Hill, the Ring Guard, with his 48-inch
coach horn, demonstrates how it is blown to
Queen Alexandra's Royal Army Nursing
Corps members Miss J.McGowan (centre)
and Miss B.Blythman.

One of the avenues lined with machinery stands which were a constant attraction to farmer and layman alike. A stand on the left is offering a tractor cab for £23 15s 0d. This was in July 1957, the year the Royal Show was held at Costessey.

Norfolk stockmen pitting their skill against the markings of the judges in the Norfolk Stockmen's Club judging competition at the Royal Show in July 1957.

Soldiers of the Royal Norfolk Regiment demonstrate a mortar to some youngsters who visited their stand.
Taking a professional interest are some Coldstream Guardsmen who were on duty at the show.

Norfolk Businesses

From the village shop to the massive bulk of Yarmouth power station, a survey of some of the businesses which make up the fabric of Norfolk. Expansion in the late 1950s and 1960s encouraged many new firms to set up shop in the county, joining traditional industries such as engineering and food processing already in existence. Here is a selection of Norfolk ventures, from the one-man band to the multi-national.

Yarmouth's new electricity generating station nearing completion at South Denes in January 1958. 160,000 tons of concrete and four million bricks were used in its construction. At 360 feet the chimney was much taller than Norwich Cathedral spire. The building closed down in 1985.

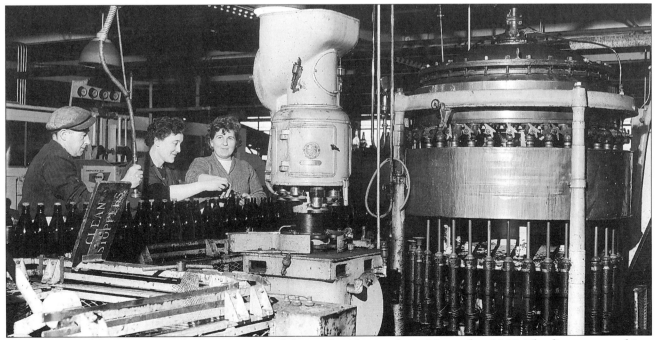

Bottles being filled and capped at Gaymer's Attleborough cider works in November 1960. The firm exported its products to 51 different countries.

Campbell's Soups' move to King's Lynn in 1959 was one of the most significant developments in Lynn's major expansion in the 1950s and 60s. Campbell's, a landmark for the thousands of drivers who travel along the nearby A47, remains one of the town's major employers. In this 1963 picture, the quality assurance department is analysing the sugar content of their soups and the consistency of the finished product.

The erecting shop where engine assembly took place at Charles Burrell's works, Thetford.

Helping to man the county's firms – and providing the next generation of entrepreneurs – is the vital role of Norfolk's education establishments. The King's Lynn Municipal Technical Institute became the County Technical College in 1956, moved into new premises on Tennyson Avenue in 1961 and has turned out thousands of students in a huge range of skills. In this 1967 picture, Mr C.Beck, lecturer, is assisting City and Guilds third year students in the motor vehicle section of the engineering department.

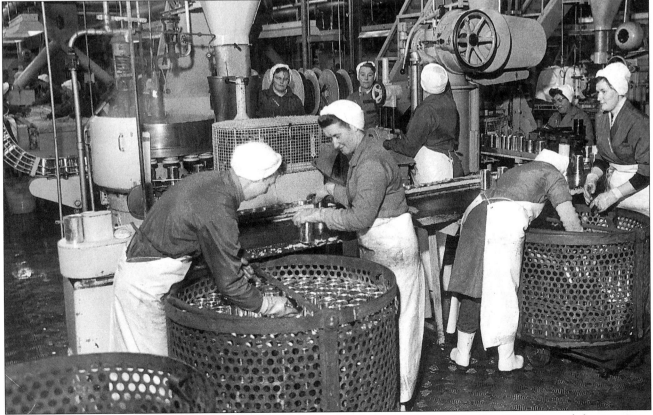

Food processing has always been a big employer in West Norfolk and Fenland. In this 1963 view of the Lin Can factory at West Lynn, workers are taking cans from a high-speed filler and loading them in crates ready to be taken to the retorts.

An old brick kiln, pictured in August 1954, which had been converted into offices by Mr D.Woolsey at Mundesley.

Jeyes Group factory under construction at the Brunel Way industrial estate, Thetford, in April 1969. It was the biggest factory yet to come to the town under the London overspill expansion scheme.

Bentinck Dock is the larger of the two docks at King's Lynn, and boasts a mile of frontage. This picture, taken on 7 June 1958, shows a British Road Services lorry with a cargo, having left its depot adjacent to the dock. In the background can be seen one of the former docks warehouses, known prosaically as R1, R2 and R3.

Children from Reedham Primary School with their Headmaster, Mr J.O.Boast, in the local church hall looking at the feathercraft coronation crown made by Pettits of Reedham in May 1953.

The village shop was as important to local people as the big department store was to townsfolk. Mr Percy Mallett pictured in September 1967, who ran The Shop on the edge of Hanworth Common, stocked tins, bottles and packets of almost everything for the household.

Norfolk Characters

In our Introduction we spoke about the Norfolk character. To finish our selection we have picked some of the 'good ol' boys' who have enriched Norfolk life. Some are famous only in their own villages or towns, two or three nationally. But all express something of that intangible specialness that is Norfolk.

The Queen doesn't only keep racehorses; she is one of the country's leading racing pigeon owners too. For many years the Royal lofts were at the modest Gaywood semi of Len Rush. Mr Rush, seen here showing some Eastern Bloc visitors round the lofts on 10 December 1970, had 18 visits from the Queen. On one occasion a neighbour knocked at the door and couldn't make anyone hear so she banged on the window instead – and was shocked to see the Queen sitting inside. Mr Rush's life was the subject of a successful biography *Captain of the Queen's Flight*.

Dick Joice, as a young lad, crammed his Great Ryburgh bedroom with clocks, speedometers and steering wheels, but it was the start of a lifelong interest in memorabilia. His unique collection of 4,000 items reflecting past crafts, professions and life-styles is admired by thousands of visitors to Holkham Hall. Life in television came from his farming when in 1958 he was invited to present *Farming Diary* for the newly-formed Anglia Television. He later presented *About Anglia* and the *Bygones* series which was screened for 20 years.

One man and his dog... a 1970 study of Reg Hare, long associated with the West Lynn ferry. The ferry provides an invaluable short cut for shoppers and commuters across the Ouse and has been plying the river in one form or another since the thirteenth century.

Far left: Although not a Norfolkman by birth – he was born in Guernsey – Ted Ellis came to live in Yarmouth at the age of 11 years. With his *In The Countryside* notes in the *Eastern Daily Press* he brought the many facets of nature to its readership. Renowned for his knowledge, he was an interesting speaker to clubs, schools, radio listeners and television viewers. His home at Wheatfen Broad, Surlingham was a naturalist's paradise, but in this March 1968 picture he is inspecting a random collection of birds which were found mysteriously dead at Ormesby.

Left: While working with a firm of auctioneers around 1950 Bernard Matthews decided to take up a profitable hobby and bought 20 turkey eggs at 1/- each together with an incubator for 30/-. His international company now rears about ten million turkeys a year and his 'bootiful' business has annual sales of more than £200 million.

Wing Commander Ken Wallis, the inventor from Reymerston, soars into the clouds with his fascinating *Little Nellie* autogyro which became famous in the James Bond films.

Keith Skipper (centre) is a champion of all things Norfolk. Through his writing and his dinner time programme on BBC Radio Norfolk he preserves the Norfolk dialect, puts the Norfolk point of view and presents the Norfolk people. Born and schooled in Norfolk, he joined the Norfolk News Company (now Eastern Counties Newspapers) as a cub reporter and worked in Thetford, Dereham, Yarmouth and Norwich. These places, together with his home in Cromer, have given him a knowledge of the county north, south, east and west. Keith is pictured with radio character 'Egbert Gladstone-Pyle' (left) and *EDP* arts and literary editor Charles Roberts.

Left: Generations of children all over the world have reason to thank the existence of this gentleman, Frederick Savage, whose statue (seen here getting a 1970 wash and brush up) stands proudly on the London Road entrance to King's Lynn. He was founder of Savage's Ltd, pioneer of steam-driven fairground roundabouts.

Right: One of the great characters of the Norfolk scene in the 1960s and 1970s was champion walker Bob Thirtle. Born near Cromer but based at King's Lynn, his career began in 1964 with 342 laps of the town's Walks park. Record walk after record walk followed; here he is in 1968 on a non-stop 179-mile trek. Bob, who at one time walked 2,000 miles a year, revealed his secret anti-blister formula in a 1977 *EDP* interview: generous applications of Friar's Balsam cough mixture.

Roger North, of Rougham Hall, starts up his 1903 De Dion Bouton at the home of the Hon Mrs Keppel of Norwich. This very car was the first to be used by the *EDP* to deliver papers between Norwich and King's Lynn.

Lady Mayhew, pictured here in August 1967, and *Pochard*, her Brown Boat, were seen frequently on the Norfolk Broads and rivers, as well as over the boundary on Oulton Broad. She was the first woman life member of the Royal Norfolk and Suffolk Yacht Club and chairman of the Broads One-Design class. In her younger days she was devoted to public work with the Girl Guide movement, the British Red Cross Society and the County Nursing Federation.

Alan Bloom's two outstanding achievements are founding a great house of gardening, Blooms of Bressingham, in 1946, and the largest live steam museum in Britain. Steam came to Bressingham in 1961 when, as a distraction from work, he bought and restored a traction engine. Here he is seen with the *Duchess of Sutherland* in March 1971.

Nonagenarian George Cushing is a man who has been in farming, road repairs, conservation and owner of Fakenham laundry. However, we are most indebted to him for his restoration of the steam traction engines and fairground organs which form the basis of his internationally-renowned Thursford Collection.

Tony Hall, the *EDP* cartoonist, whose caricatures of people – local, national and international – have brought a smile to readers' faces since 1977. His other talent, playing an ageing melodeon while singing folk songs and sea shanties, brings him into the public eye around the county.

Bespectacled Grimsby postman Allan Smethurst shot to fame in 1965 as the Singing Postman when he released two EPs of dialect songs about his childhood near Sheringham. By April 1965 – when this picture was taken at a signing session at Wheeler's record store, King's Lynn, his records were number 1 and 3 in the local charts, outselling The Seekers, The Animals, Manfred Mann, Cliff Richard – and the Beatles.

Subscribers

Mrs H J Allcock
Mrs H J Allcock
Frank Allen
M E Allen
Wally & Olive Ashby
Walter Atkins
Mrs June Axtell
Mr & Mrs D A Baker
Margaret Baker
Michael John Banham
Eileen Banyard & James Glover
Mrs J E Barnard
June & John Barnard
R N Barrett
Joyce R Batchelor APAGB
Henry Baugh-Ward
Mr E J Bell
D R Benson
Mr & Mrs Benton
Mr M A Betts
Mr & Mrs W Bloy
Mr C Boldero
Mr & Mrs D Bowman
Tony Bradstreet
Mr T E B Braddock
Richard James Brady
Gillian Bray
Doreen & Ray Breeze
D R Bright
V R Brockwell
Paul Brown
Mr & Mrs Brudenell
Alan & Margaret Buckel
Michael Bullivant
J & H Bunn Ltd
W E Burcham
D Burdett
Daphne R Burnham
Derek Buxton
Paul Bye
Mrs A Cain
Barry Caley
Mrs R V Calton
Mr G Canfer
Anthony Ernest Cannell
Michael Capocci
Andrew J Carter
Mr D R Carter
Mr & Mrs F A Carter

Keith & Patricia Carvell
Zoe Chandler
Elizabeth Chaplin
Roy & Frances Chaplin
Mrs Margaret Chapman
Mr Norman A Church
Glen & Mary Clarke
Roy R W Clarke
Mr W E Cook
Gill & Terence Copley
G A Copping
Brenda Copsey
John Creasey
Mr B & Mrs K E Crisp
Mr B & Mrs K E Crisp
Mrs Nicola Crossman
Mr P G & Mrs L A Daniels
Mrs Beryl M D'Arcy
Mr H W Davison
Peter C P Day
Edward A J Dell
Mrs E V Dewart
R G Dickerson
Mr B Dickinson
June & Eric Drake
R B Dryland
T D Eagling
Mr T East
Miss L M Eden
Mrs J Emery
Mrs M K Faircloth
Ron & Joy Farman
T J Fiddy
A G Firrell
Mrs K Fiscus
Phyllis Flint
Phyllis Flint
Arthur Flowerdew
R & J Flowerdew
Clare L Forbes
Dr C M Ford
Mr & Mrs D B Forgan
Pauline Foster
Mr R W Franklin
Ethel V Freeman
Ethel V Freeman
Ethel V Freeman
G J French
L E Gallaugher

Mr K Gant
John F Garrood
Revd Philip & Mrs Alice Gee
Mr Jack George
Vic & Hilda Gibbons
Marion Gissing
E W Gittins
Mr R D Gooch
Lorraine Greatbatch
John Green
Raymond Green
John Grey
Mr D L Griffin
David Richard Gubbin
C E Gunton
Mrs Bridget A Hall
Mrs Bridget A Hall
F D Hall
H C Hall
Mrs K M Harrold
Mrs A Harsant
H Harvey
H Harvey
Mr W Hawes
John Hayes
Ruth Hayes
P J Hickling
Mrs Dawne Victoria Hill
Glen Hipperson
Mrs I Holmes
Kathleen Mary Holmes
Eva Houchen
Mr & Mrs Howard
David W Howard
John E Howard
Robert E Howard
Stephen A Howard
Pauline Hudspith
Tom & Trish Hughes
Keith George Hugman
John R Hunter
Walter Hurn
Peter Jacobs
R Jarvis
Gerald Jermany
J N Jonas
Mr & Mrs G Keeley
Mrs Margaret L Ketteringham
Dr I F Keymer
Mrs J S Kiddell
J M & C P King
John & Christine Lakin

Mr & Mrs T Land
Michael Landfear
Robert & Susan Langley
Mark Andrew Larter
Diane Laver
Bernard Leighton
Mr & Mrs G H Le Surf
R G Light
Daniel Lilly
Mark Lilly
Mr & Mrs James B Little
David Lockwood
Mrs C S Long
David & Muriel Lyon
Mrs H Loasby
Mrs Pauline Anne Mabbitt
Arthur McCarthy
Mrs B B Mann
F B Manning
John S Marshall
David Martin
Mr & Mrs J P F Mason
Enid Matthews
Colin & Mary Meaden
Bernice Melton
R J Melton
Ken & Jean Miller
Roger W Mills
Ted & Gwen Moody
Mr J V Moore
Mr A C Morter
John David Morton
Simon P Murphy
Pamela Naulls
Sheila Neave
Mrs M Neal
Miss M Newell
Hazel & Bryan Norfolk
E W & M E Norman
Les & Yvonne Orbell
Mrs C E Osborn
Mrs A Osborne
Mr J Otway
Mr & Mrs Ken Ottoway
Bruce Page
Mr H Page
Susan Page
Mrs A H Palmer
G G Pardon
Shirley Peeling
David Penny
David A Perryman

Mrs Agnes Pieksma

Mrs N R Pigg

John & Joan Pitchers

Alan Pollard

Mrs Pamela Poole

Mrs Pamela Poole

Mrs D E Pfeil

Andrew Price

Jack Pritty

Ann Pulford

Mr E W Pursey

Mr M Ray

Wendy Reynolds

Mrs Daphne D Riches

Frederick D Rix

Robin Roberson

Robin Roberson

Myrtle & Derek Roberts

Susan Robichaud

Mrs O B Robinson

The Rought Family

Jack & Margaret Rounce

Mr I Rowarth

Rodney J Sanders

Peter B Sayer

Robert F E Scott

J R Secker

Mr Albert Sexton

Mrs Delma E Sherman

Deborah Shillingford

Mr Adrian Short

Mrs M Shotton

Ray Shreeve

John Sillett

Joyce Sillett

Roger Simmons

Mrs M Skidmore

Brian Herbert Smith

Ian L Smith

Ron Smith

Roy Smith

Tony Smith

M Southerland

M Southerland

Mrs J Sowerby

Ron Spall

Mrs A Sparrow

Edgar C Spelman

Mrs J Spinks

Mrs N Stagg

M & M A Stansfield

B C Starkey

M J Starkey

Don Stevens

Mr R T Stevens

Christine Stone

John Stubbert

Mrs B M Sturgess

Mr & Mrs Alfred A Sugalski

John Swain

J M Swatman

K W Taylor

Mr M A Taylor

William Taylor

Mr S Tebbutt

H & A Terry

Mrs J Terry

David Thornhill

Richard Thornhill

Peter Threadkell

C E Trory

Nigel Lewis Turner

Marcus Van Nieuwkerk

R C Walpole

Jean & John Ward

June Edwina Wasey

J Waterson

Mr & Mrs W R Watkinson

G C Watling

Mr D W Watts

M W & C N Watts

B Weston

B Weston

Mrs Myrle White

Mrs Myrle White

David Whiteside

Roger Whiting

G B Whitlam

Brenda Williams

Peter Williamson

Maurice Wilson

Peter Wiltshire

Mrs J C Windows

Peter Winter

Robert Woodcock

D Woods

Ruth & Alf Wooltorton

Dominic Wren

R & B E Wright

Mrs A Yallop

Margaret Yaxley

Mr H Young

Rachel Young